Weekly Reader Books presents

What to do when your mom or dad says . . .
"BE GOOD WHILE YOU'RE THERE!"

By

JOY WILT BERRY

Living Skills Press
Fallbrook, California

CREDITS

Producer
  Ron Berry

Editor
  Orly Kelly

Copyright © 1982 Joy Wilt Berry
All rights reserved.
Printed in the United States of America.
Library of Congress Catalog Card Number: 82-81202
ISBN 0-941510-07-7

Weekly Reader Books edition published by
arrangement with Living Skills Press.

Dear Parents:

"BE GOOD WHILE YOU'RE THERE!" Have you ever said this to your child and had him or her ask you, "Why?"

You could answer this question by saying, "Because I told you so!" But there really is a better answer.

This whole issue is a matter of etiquette. Etiquette is not an "optional part of the program." In situations involving relationships, etiquette is essential.

Etiquette is the guideline that shows us how to act in pleasing and acceptable ways. It tells us how to be gracious around other people.

Sound etiquette is based on three very important principles.

The first is: DO UNTO OTHERS AS YOU WOULD HAVE THEM DO UNTO YOU. Every one of us has a deep need to be treated with kindness and respect. If we hope to receive this kindness and respect from other people, we must treat them with kindness and respect. Centered in this truth is the balance between "what's good for me" and "what's good for you" which is necessary for the survival and growth of any human relationship.

The second principle is: BEAUTY IS AS BEAUTY DOES. This means that our personal beauty depends on our behavior rather than our physical appearance. In other words, it is how we act rather than how we appear which makes us ugly or beautiful. No matter what we look like, crude behavior can turn us into something ugly, while gracious behavior can make us beautiful in a very special way.

The third principle is: A THING OF BEAUTY IS A JOY FOREVER! Think about it. When you are around something that is ugly, you probably feel sad and depressed. On the other hand, when you are around something that is beautiful, you probably feel inspired and happy.

It is the same way with people.

Being around a person who is ugly because of crude behavior is often sad and depressing. However, being around a person who is beautiful because of gracious behavior is often inspiring and uplifting.

Generally speaking, people do not want to be around a person who makes them feel depressed. Instead, they want to be around someone who makes them feel good.

Being gracious will most likely make others desire rather than resist your companionship, and this is important as all of us are social beings.

Your child comes into the world as a social being possessing specific social needs. Accompanying these needs are your child's innate abilities to get his or her needs met, but these abilities are undeveloped. One of your jobs as a parent is to facilitate the development of these abilities. You can accomplish this by doing these things:

1. Help your child observe and evaluate his or her own behavior as it relates to others.

2. Bring your child into a basic understanding of the three principles mentioned above.

3. Help your child clarify social expectations.

4. Expose your child to guidelines which can enable him or her to meet valid social expectations.

This book can help you achieve all four of these things. If you will use it systematically (as part of a continuing program) or as a resource (to be used whenever the need for it arises), you and your child will experience some very positive results.

With your help, your child can and will know exactly what you mean when you say "BE GOOD WHILE YOU'RE THERE!" and will be able to respond in a gracious way.

Sincerely,

Joy Wilt Berry

Has your mother or father ever told you to …

When your mom or dad says, "Be good while you're there!" do you ever wonder …

If any of this sounds familiar to you, you're going to **love** this book.

Because this book is going to tell you exactly what to do when you visit someone.

BEING INVITED TO SOMEONE'S HOME

This is Ida Impolite.

Ida Impolite never waits to be invited to a person's house or apartment. Instead, she "drops in" whenever she pleases. Ida is not very gracious.

Whenever you have been invited for a visit, you can be gracious by doing these things:

1. Wait to be invited or call ahead of time and get permission before you go to another person's house or apartment.

2. Make sure that both your parents and the other person's parents approve of the visit before you go.

3. After you receive an invitation, find out as soon as possible whether or not you can go.

4. Let the person who has invited you know as soon as possible if and when you will be coming.

5. Make sure both of you are clear on the exact time you will be arriving and leaving.

6. If you accept a person's invitation, **show up** and **be on time** unless there is an emergency which prevents you from doing so.

WHEN YOU APPROACH SOMEONE'S DOOR

Whenever Ida Impolite knocks on a door or rings a doorbell, she does it continuously until the door is opened.

Whenever someone opens the door, Ida Impolite rushes into the house or apartment without waiting to be invited in. Once she is inside, Ida sits down before being offered a seat. Ida is not very gracious.

Whenever you approach someone's door, you can be gracious by doing these things:

1. Try the doorbell first. Ring it once and give the person inside enough time to get to the door. If there is no response, ring the doorbell a second time. (Do not keep your finger on the bell for a very long time.)

2. If there is no response after the second ring, knock on the door. Again, give the person a chance to get to the door. (Do not knock too loudly and do not knock more than twice.)

If there is no answer, do not look into the house through the windows to see if anyone is home. If a person does not answer the door, it is because no one is home or wants to talk to anyone. You need to respect this.

3. When someone opens the door, wait to be invited in before you walk in.

   If the other person forgets to invite you in, it is appropriate for you to say, "May I come in?"

4. If you are wearing a wet raincoat and/or boots, remove them before you come into the house provided that there is some shelter where you can do this. Also leave your wet umbrella outside or ask if there is a specific place for wet umbrellas inside the house.

If your shoes are dirty or muddy, clean them off before you walk into the house or apartment.

BEFORE I COME IN I'D BETTER TAKE MY RAINGEAR OFF AND LEAVE IT OUTSIDE SO I DON'T GET EVERYTHING WET AND MUDDY.

VISITING OTHER PEOPLE IN THEIR HOMES

Whenever Ida Impolite visits another person's home, she is disrespectful. She expects everyone in the family to revolve all of their activities around her and to wait on her hand and foot.

Whenever Ida Impolite visits another person's home, she forgets to get permission to use things and often ends up damaging or destroying them.

Whenever you visit another person's home, you can be gracious by doing these things:

1. Treat every person and pet in the household with kindness and respect.

2. Follow the rules and schedule of the household, even though they might be different from the ones at your house.

3. Cooperate enthusiastically with the activities that the family and/or other person has planned and suggest things to do only when you are asked.

4. Do not go into any room in the house or get into any drawer, closet, etc., without permission.

5. Do not use anything (including the telephone, TV, radio, food, etc.) without permission.

6. Do not ask anyone to give you anything you
   see and would like to keep for yourself.

7. Be careful with the things you use. Do not damage or destroy them.

8. If you should damage or destroy something, say so immediately. Say you are sorry and do whatever you can to make up for the damage.

9. Put anything you use back in its proper place when you are finished using it. Clean up every mess you make right after you make it. A good rule is, "Don't put it down; put it away."

10. Do not eat any food without its first being offered to you. When food is offered, do not be greedy. Take only your share.

11. Leave exactly when you planned to leave. Don't overstay your welcome.

12. Remember to thank your friend and his or her parents before you leave.

HAVING SOMEONE IN YOUR HOME

When Randy Rude has someone in his home, he often ignores the person. He expects the person to entertain himself or herself.

When Randy Rude isn't neglecting his guests, he is bossing them around. If the other person does not do exactly what Randy wants, Randy tells the person to go home.

Whenever you visit someone for a short period of time, you can be gracious by doing these things:

1. Do not stay too long. Make sure that your visit does not interfere with your friend's dinner hour or with the things your friend's parents want him or her to do.

2. Take turns visiting. Once you have visited someone's home, invite him or her to your home. Don't always be the visitor. It's fun to be the host or hostess, too.

SPENDING THE NIGHT

Whenever Ida Impolite spends the night at someone's home, she forgets to bring the things she needs and has to borrow them. In addition, she hogs the bathroom.

Ida Impolite never picks up after herself and never cleans up the messes she makes. Ida is not very gracious.

Whenever you visit a person for a long period of time, you can be gracious by doing these things:

1. Bring everything you need (suitable clothing, toothbrush, toothpaste, shampoo, brush, comb, etc.) so that you will not have to borrow anything from the family you are visiting. Generally speaking, they will provide soap, towels, and bedding for you, but you should offer to bring your sleeping bag and pillow in case they do not have extra bedding.

2. Put your things away when you arrive, if a space has been made available to you for this purpose.

3. Eat the food that is served. Do not expect anyone to prepare special food for you. Make requests only if you are asked.

4. Do not spend more time than necessary in the bathroom, if it must be shared with someone else.

5. Clean up after yourself. Help with the dishes. Make your own bed; pick up your own clothes. Clean up the tub, shower, and sink after you use them, and hang up the bath towels you use.

6. When you leave, be sure to take home everything you brought.

And remember, if you want to be a visitor who will be asked back again and again, always treat the people you visit the same way you wish they would treat you. If you do this, you'll always do the right thing.

THE END of not knowing what to do when you
get there.